ME

Food

You're The Greatest, Charlie Brown

Charles M. Schulz

Selected Cartoons from
AS YOU LIKE IT, CHARLIE BROWN Vol. II

CORONET BOOKS
Hodder Fawcett Ltd., London

Printed and bound in Great Britain for
Coronet Books,
Hodder Fawcett Ltd,
St. Paul's House, Warwick Lane,
London, EC4P 4AH
by Hazell Watson & Viney Ltd,
Aylesbury, Bucks

ISBN 0 340 15135 8

DEAR SANTA CLAUS,
I AM WRITING IN BEHALF OF MY DOG, SNOOPY. HE IS A GOOD DOG.

IN FACT, I'LL BET IF ONE OF YOUR REINDEER EVER GOT SICK, SNOOPY WOULD FILL IN FOR HIM, AND HELP PULL YOUR SLED.

AHEM!

WELL, PERHAPS NOT. BUT HE'S STILL A GOOD DOG IN MANY WAYS.

GOOD GRIEF!

DID THE LITTLE BOY WHO SITS IN FRONT OF YOU AT SCHOOL CRY AGAIN TODAY?

HE CRIES EVERY DAY! HE HAS ALL THE SIMPLE CHILDHOOD FEARS...FEAR OF BEING LATE FOR SCHOOL, FEAR OF HIS TEACHER, AND FEAR OF THE PRINCIPAL...

FEAR OF NOT KNOWING WHAT ROOM TO GO TO AFTER RECESS, FEAR OF FORGETTING HIS LUNCH, FEAR OF BIGGER KIDS, FEAR OF BEING ASKED TO RECITE...

FEAR OF MISSING THE SCHOOL BUS, FEAR OF NOT KNOWING WHEN TO GET OFF THE SCHOOL BUS, FEAR OF...

GOOD GRIEF!

LUCY VOLUNTEERED ME TO SING "JINGLE BELLS" AT THE PTA CHRISTMAS PROGRAM..

I CAN'T SING IN PUBLIC! I'M A **TERRIBLE** SINGER! I NEVER **HAVE** BEEN ABLE TO SING!

DON'T WORRY ABOUT IT... IN PSALM 98 WE READ, "MAKE A JOYFUL NOISE UNTO THE LORD"

THIS IS THE PTA!!

I'VE GOT IT ALL FIGURED OUT...

INSTEAD OF SINGING, SNOOPY AND I ARE GOING TO GIVE 'EM THE "JINGLE BELL TWIST"....

YOU'RE NOT!

I KNOW WHEN TO LEAVE..

YOU THOUGHT YOU COULD PULL A FAST ONE, DIDN'T YOU?

YOU THOUGHT YOU COULD GO OUT THERE IN FRONT OF THE WHOLE PTA, AND SLIP IN A LITTLE SERMON, DIDN'T YOU?

THOU SPEAKEST HARSH WORDS AT YULETIDE!

Merry Christmas!

HAVE YOU EVER HEARD OF A DIATRYMA?

HE WAS A BIRD WHO STOOD SEVEN FEET TALL AND HAD A HEAD AS LARGE AS THAT OF A HORSE! HE HAD A HUGE SHARP BILL AND POWERFUL LEGS WITH WHICH HE COULD RUN DOWN SMALL ANIMALS

HE IS NOW EXTINCT... IN FACT, HE HASN'T BEEN AROUND FOR SIXTY BILLION YEARS...

AND WE DON'T MISS HIM A BIT!

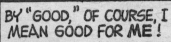

WE HAVE TO WRITE A BOOK REPORT ON "PETER RABBIT" FOR SCHOOL..

I'M GOING TO MAKE A CHARACTER ANALYSIS OF THE FARMER IN THE STORY...YOU KNOW, TRY TO POINT UP HIS BASIC ATTITUDES TOWARD RABBITS, AND SO ON...

I MAY EVEN BRING IN SOME SPECULATIONS ON HIS HOME LIFE WHICH COULD PROVE TO BE QUITE INTERESTING...

ALL IN ALL I HOPE TO UNCOVER SOME NEW TRUTHS ABOUT OUR CULTURE..

I THINK YOU ALREADY HAVE!

BOY, YOU LOOK TERRIBLE, CHARLIE BROWN...

YOU LOOK LIKE YOU'VE BEEN TAKING SHOCK TREATMENTS OR SOMETHING..

WHAT'S MORE SHOCKING THAN SEEING YOUR FAULTS PROJECTED ON A SCREEN?

I FEEL TERRIBLE!

IT COST ME TEN DOLLARS TO RENT THE SLIDE PROJECTOR..

IT COST ME ANOTHER THIRTY-THREE DOLLARS TO HAVE THE SLIDES MADE UP...THAT TOTALS TO FORTY-THREE DOLLARS...

THE ONE HUNDRED DOLLARS IS MY PERSONAL FEE...SO ALL IN ALL YOU OWE ME $143.00

AND I STILL HAVE THE SAME FAULTS!

BOOT!

HUMANE SOCIETY

THERE'S THAT LITTLE RED-HAIRED GIRL...SHE'S HANDING OUT VALENTINES..

SHE'S HANDING THEM OUT TO ALL HER FRIENDS...SHE'S HANDING THEM OUT ONE BY ONE...SHE'S HANDING THEM OUT..SHE'S STILL HANDING THEM OUT..

NOW SHE'S ALL DONE...THAT WAS THE LAST ONE...NOW SHE'S WALKING AWAY...

HAPPY VALENTINE'S DAY!

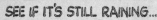
SEE IF IT'S STILL RAINING...

I CAN'T TELL..MY ARMS ARE TOO SHORT!

HAPPINESS IS A
SIDE-DISH OF FRENCH FRIES!

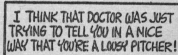

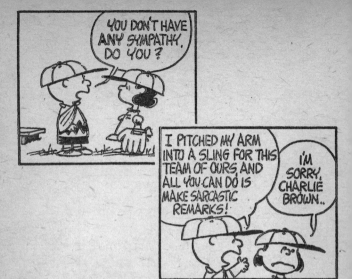

OKAY, LINUS... YOU'RE GOING TO HAVE TO DO THE PITCHING FOR AWHILE..

NOW, I DON'T WANT YOU TO GET "LITTLE LEAGUER'S ELBOW," TOO, SO WARM UP SLOWLY...JUST THROW SMOOTH AND EASY...AND ABSOLUTELY NO CURVE BALLS!

WHAT'LL I DO WITH MY BLANKET?

I'LL HOLD IT FOR YOU

YOU'RE A GOOD MANAGER, CHARLIE BROWN!

I'D LIKE TO WRITE A PAMPHLET OR SOMETHING..

I'D LIKE TO TELL EVERY KID WHO PLAYS BASEBALL HOW NOT TO GET "LITTLE LEAGUER'S ELBOW"... AND I'D ESPECIALLY LIKE TO TELL THEIR ADULT MANAGERS AND COACHES

KIDS OUR AGE OR EVEN OLDER JUST AREN'T DEVELOPED ENOUGH TO THROW A BALL HARD INNING AFTER INNING..

MAYBE THAT'S OUR TROUBLE... OUR INNINGS ARE TOO LONG !

DEAR PENCIL-PAL,
THIS IS THE FIRST DAY
I HAVE HAD MY ARM OUT
OF A SLING.

I HAVE BEEN SUFFERING
FROM "LITTLE LEAGUER'S ELBOW."

IT WAS VERY
PAINFUL.

FOR ME, THAT IS.
NOT MY TEAM !!!

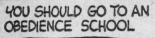

WE'RE GOING TO HAVE A SCIENCE FAIR AT SCHOOL... I'D SURE LIKE TO WIN A RIBBON..

I'VE GOT TO COME UP WITH SOME KIND OF PROJECT THAT WILL BE SO ORIGINAL AND SO DIFFERENT THAT I'LL BE CERTAIN TO WIN!

ALL THE OTHER KIDS WILL HAVE ROCKS AND BUGS AND BATTERIES AND MICE AND SEEDS AND ALL OF THAT STUFF...I'VE GOT TO THINK OF SOMETHING COMPLETELY DIFFERENT..

THAT'S IT!

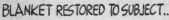

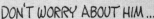

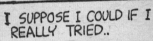

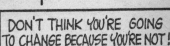

DEAR PENCIL PAL,
WELL, I MADE A FOOL
OUT OF MYSELF AGAIN.

SIGH

I STRUCK OUT WITH
THE BASES LOADED,
AND LOST THE BALL GAME.

A LITTLE RED-HAIRED
GIRL WHOM I ADMIRE VERY
MUCH WAS WATCHING ME.

COULD YOU TELL ME HOW TO
GET TO WHERE YOU LIVE?
I'M THINKING OF LEAVING
THE COUNTRY!

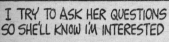

THERE! I PLAYED IT ALL THE WAY THROUGH WITHOUT A SINGLE MISTAKE!

LUCK!